Endorsements for the Flourish Bible Study Series

"The brilliant and beautiful mix of sound teaching, helpful charts, lists, sidebars, and appealing graphics—as well as insightful questions that get the reader into the text of Scripture—makes these studies that women will want to invest time in and will look back on as time well spent."

Nancy Guthrie, Bible teacher; author, *Even Better than Eden*

"My daughter and I love using Flourish Bible Studies for our morning devotions. Lydia Brownback's faithful probing of biblical texts; insightful questions; invitations to engage in personal applications using additional biblical texts and historical contexts; and commitment to upholding the whole counsel of God as it bears on living life as a godly woman have drawn us closer to the Lord and to his word. Brownback never sidesteps hard questions or hard providences, but neither does she appeal to discourses of victimhood or therapy, which are painfully common in the genre of women's Bible studies. I cannot recommend this series highly enough. My daughter and I look forward to working through this whole series together!"

Rosaria Butterfield, Former Professor of English, Syracuse University; author, *The Gospel Comes with a House Key*

"As a women's ministry leader, I am excited about the development of the Flourish Bible Study series, which will not only prayerfully equip women to increase in biblical literacy but also come alongside them to build a systematic and comprehensive framework to become lifelong students of the word of God. This series provides visually engaging studies with accessible content that will not only strengthen the believer but the church as well."

Karen Hodge, Coordinator of Women's Ministries, Presbyterian Church in America; coauthor, *Transformed*

"Lydia Brownback is an experienced Bible teacher who has dedicated her life to ministry roles that help women (and men) grow in Christ. With a wealth of biblical, historical, and theological content, her Flourish Bible Studies are ideal for groups and individuals that are serious about the in-depth study of the word of God."

Phil and Lisa Ryken, President, Wheaton College; and his wife, Lisa

"If you're looking for rich, accessible, and deeply biblical Bible studies, this series is for you! Lydia Brownback leads her readers through different books of the Bible, providing background information, maps, timelines, and questions that probe the text in order to glean understanding and application. She settles us deeply in the context of a book as she highlights God's unfolding plan of redemption and rescue. You will learn, you will delight in God's word, and you will love our good King Jesus even more."

Courtney Doctor, Coordinator of Women's Initiatives, The Gospel Coalition; author, *From Garden to Glory* and *Steadfast*

T0339257

"Lydia Brownback's Bible study series provides a faithful guide to book after book. You'll find rich insights into context and good questions to help you study and interpret the Bible. Page by page, the studies point you to respond to each passage and to love our great and gracious God. I will recommend the Flourish series for years to come for those looking for a wise, Christ-centered study that leads toward the goal of being transformed by the word."

Taylor Turkington, Bible teacher; Director, BibleEquipping.org

"Lydia Brownback has a contagious love for the Bible. Not only is she fluent in the best of biblical scholarship in the last generation, but her writing is accessible to the simplest of readers. She has the rare ability of being clear without being reductionistic. I anticipate many women indeed will flourish through her trustworthy guidance in this series."

David Mathis, Senior Teacher and Executive Editor, desiringGod.org; Pastor, Cities Church, Saint Paul, Minnesota; author, *Habits of Grace*

"Lydia Brownback's Flourish Bible Study series has been a huge gift to the women's ministry in my local church. Many of our groups have gone through her studies in both the Old and New Testaments and have benefited greatly. The Flourish Bible Study series is now my go-to for a combination of rich Bible study, meaningful personal application, and practical group interaction. I recommend them whenever a partner in ministry asks me for quality women's Bible study resources. I'm so thankful Brownback continues to write them and share them with us!"

Jen Oshman, author, *Enough about Me* and *Cultural Counterfeits*; Women's Ministry Coordinator, Redemption Parker, Colorado

JAMES

Flourish Bible Study Series
By Lydia Brownback

FLOURISH
BIBLE STUDY

JAMES

WALKING IN WISDOM

LYDIA BROWNBACK

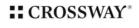

WHEATON, ILLINOIS

Crossway is a publishing ministry of Good News Publishers.

RRDS   33 32 31 30 29 28 27 26 25 24
16 15 14 13 12 11 10 9 8 7 6 5 4 3

With gratitude to God
for
Laura Layer,
who lives a Christ-centered, single-minded life

CONTENTS

THE TIMING
OF JAMES

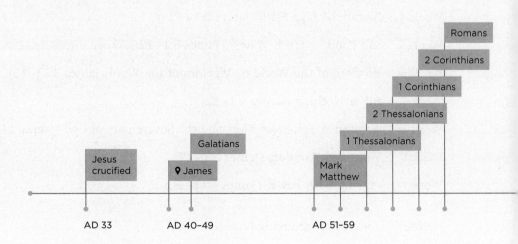

Jesus
crucified

Galatians

📍 James

Mark
Matthew

1 Thessalonians

2 Thessalonians

1 Corinthians

2 Corinthians

Romans

AD 33   AD 40–49   AD 51–59

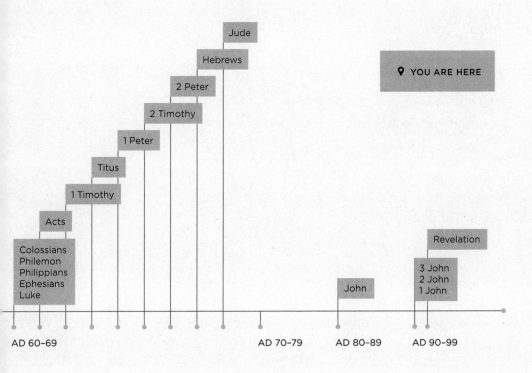

Jude

Hebrews

2 Peter

2 Timothy

1 Peter

Titus

1 Timothy

Acts

Colossians
Philemon
Philippians
Ephesians
Luke

📍 YOU ARE HERE

Revelation

3 John
2 John
1 John

John

AD 60–69   AD 70–79   AD 80–89   AD 90–99

INTRODUCTION

GETTING INTO JAMES

A lost phone, a twisted ankle, a juice stain on the couch—what a day can bring! We usually know by breakfast if it's going to be one of those days, but we press ahead, determined to hold irritability in check and count our blessings. After all, we tell ourselves, it's not like we're facing a major crisis. When the crises do come, they knock our comparatively minor problems to the edge of the bad-day spectrum. Even so, whether big or small, major or minor, our difficulties make life, well, difficult. James shows us how to makes sense of the struggles we face and how to trust God more fully in the midst of them. And that's just the beginning of his letter! Down to earth and practical—that's why James's epistle is among the most loved in the New Testament. In some ways, it reads a lot like the proverbs in the Old Testament—short, snappy bits of instruction and guidance mixed in with life-saving warnings. James paints colorful word pictures too, from storm-tossed seas to the gentle rains that make crops grow. Down through the centuries, some theologians have been wary of this epistle. That's because James seems to write very little about Christ and the gospel. But as we will see, James's letter drives us straight to the gospel and helps us embrace it. Even though James doesn't say much about the person and work of Jesus, no New Testament letter is more influenced by Jesus's teaching than the letter James wrote.[1] As we study it over the next ten weeks, we'll come to know our Lord better, and we will love him more. Plus we can't help but come away with a renewed zeal for discipleship and walking closely with our Lord in every facet of our lives.

AUTHOR

James the brother of Jesus is the author of the letter that bears his name. Back in his day, he was known as James the Just because he had a passion for righteousness. No one is completely sure when James came to believe his half-brother was the Son of God. The Gospels tell us that Jesus's brothers were skeptics while they were all growing up together in the same household (Mark 3:20–21; John 7:2–5). But much later, after Jesus

---

Pronunciation Guide

Abraham: AY-bra-ham   **Isaac:** EYE-zick   **Rahab:** RAY-hab

Elijah: EE-lie-ja   **James:** Jaymes   **Job:** Jobe

---

had died and was raised from death, he appeared to James in a special way (see 1 Corinthians 15:7), and James's faith became evident all through the early church. In fact, James became a well-known leader in the church at Jerusalem (Acts 15:13–21 and Galatians 2:9 provide a glimpse of his authority). Although he was not one of the original apostles, he is linked with them, and the apostle Paul refers to James as an apostle (Galatians 1:19). James died during the early years of the church, in AD 62.

The Setting of James

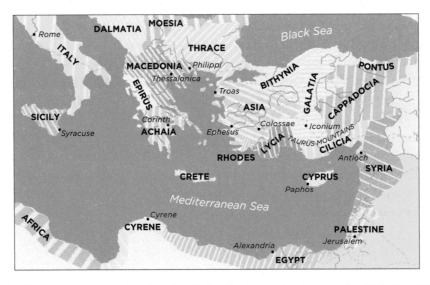

The epistle of James was written primarily to Jewish Christian house churches outside of Palestine. This would mean it was sent throughout most of the ancient Mediterranean world.[2]

SETTING

The original readers of James's letter were Jewish Christians. They'd grown up knowing the law of Moses and then had heard the gospel and put their faith in Jesus Christ for salvation. James wrote the letter during the early years of the fledgling church, sometime during the mid-40s. Most likely, these believers made up a group of house churches outside of Palestine.

THEMES

Dealing with difficulty is a theme threaded all through the letter. It seems that James's original readers were experiencing hardship because of their faith, and James wants to help them know how to make sense of it. He explains where God is—and isn't—when believers experience tests, trials, and temptations of all kinds. Overarching everything he writes is his teaching about faith—faith is proven to be genuine when it is backed up by deeds or good works. Genuine religion, James says, can be seen by our words, the things we say, as well as how we treat the poor and marginalized. And guarding our hearts against worldly influence is another mark of genuine godliness. The problem is, none of us measures up to these marks, so James calls us to humble ourselves, submit to God, and experience the power of his forgiving, transforming grace.

"Basic to all that James says in his letter is his concern that his readers stop compromising with worldly values and behavior and give themselves wholly to the Lord. Spiritual wholeness . . . is the central concern of the letter."[3]

STUDYING JAMES

At the beginning of each week's lesson, read the entire passage. And then read it again. If you are studying James with a group, read it once more, aloud, when you gather to discuss the lesson. *Marinating in the Scripture text is the most important part of any Bible study.*

GROUP STUDY

If you are doing this study as part of a group, you'll want to finish each week's lesson before the group meeting. You can work your way through the study questions all in one sitting or by doing a little bit each day. And don't be discouraged if you don't have sufficient time to answer every question. Just do as much as you can, knowing that the more you do, the more you'll learn. No matter how much of the study you are able to complete each week, the group will benefit simply from your presence, so don't skip the gathering if you can't finish! That being said, group time will be most rewarding for every participant if you have done the lesson in advance.

If you are leading the group, you can download the leader's tips at https://www.lydiabrownback.com/flourish-series.

INDIVIDUAL STUDY

The study is designed to run for ten weeks, but you can set your own pace if you're studying solo. And you can download the leader's tips (https://www.lydiabrownback.com/flourish-series) if you'd like some guidance along the way.

*Marinating in the Scripture text is the
most important part of any Bible study.*

Reading Plan

	Primary Text	Supplemental Reading
Week 1	James 1:1–18	Genesis 22:1–14
Week 2	James 1:19–27	Ephesians 4:17–24
Week 3	James 2:1–13	Leviticus 25:35–38; Matthew 7:12
Week 4	James 2:14–26	Genesis 15:1–6; 22:1–14; Joshua 2:1–21; 6:15–25; Hebrews 11:31
Week 5	James 3:1–12	Matthew 12:33–37; 15:18–19
Week 6	James 3:13–18	Philippians 2:3–11
Week 7	James 4:1–12	Leviticus 19:9–18; Matthew 7:7–11
Week 8	James 4:13–17	Psalm 90; Luke 12:15–21
Week 9	James 5:1–12	Psalm 37; Matthew 6:19–21
Week 10	James 5:13–20	James 4:6–10

BETTER THAN WARM AND FUZZY

JAMES 1:1–18

A friend of mine was referred to a fertility specialist in order to determine why she'd been unable to conceive a child. Before going, she was given a word of caution about the specialist: "She's really good, but she's very blunt, so don't expect warm and fuzzy." The advice was on point, because the first thing that the specialist told my friend after a battery of tests was, "If you're here because you want children, there's nothing I can do for you." Because my friend had been prepared, she didn't collapse in tears right then and there. And mixed in with her very natural grief, she actually felt a measure of relief that she finally had a definitive answer and could get on with planning her future. She was thankful for the specialist, not only for her expertise but also for her direct approach. Well, James is a bit like that specialist—blunt and to the point. He uses few words in powerful ways, not just once but over and over again. We see it right at the outset. Immediately after the briefest of greetings, he gives instructions that must have felt initially like a slap in the face to some of his readers: *Link your hardships—your pain, grief, unfair treatment, disappointment, and deprivation—to joy*, he says, in so many words. *It's these very hardships*, he adds, *that make you a strong, committed believer*. Ouch! But just like the medical specialist who helped my friend, James's words and their initially painful impact are meant to set us free and lead us into a bright future. That's what we'll examine this week. We'll also learn how to tell the difference between tests of faith and temptations to sin—a vital distinction. No matter how long we've walked with Christ, we never outgrow our need of what James teaches us this week.

1. WHO'S WHO IN JAMES (1:1)

We learn a good bit about James and those to whom he's writing in the very first verse, where he greets "the twelve tribes in the Dispersion." The Christians receiving his letter have a heritage that goes back to the twelve tribes of Israel, the people of God whose story unfolds in the Old Testament. This heritage is much richer and fuller now that they have been united to Christ by faith. Over the centuries, the original twelve tribes had been scattered—dispersed—all over the known world, but those who'd come to know Christ were being regathered in a whole new way as the early church formed and got established.

✦ In light of the fact that James was not only a brother of Jesus but had also become one of the most prominent leaders of the early church (noted for you in the introduction), what is significant about how he introduces himself in verse 1? In other words, what does his introduction reveal about his character?

2. THE ADVANTAGES OF ADVERSITY (1:2-8)

James instructs his friends to "count it all joy" when trials come (v. 2). He's not suggesting that Christians are supposed to paste on a happy face and pretend nothing is wrong. His counsel has to do with perspective. When a difficulty comes, we want to be realistic about how bad it is, but in the very midst of it, we shift our gaze from our trouble to God and his purposes.

✦ According to verse 3, what is happening to our faith when we experience trials?

✦ The intended outcome of believers' trials is *steadfastness* (v. 3). Your Bible translation might use *endurance* or *perseverance* instead of *steadfastness*. What is the long-term impact of steadfastness on God's people?

✦ James encourages sufferers to pray for wisdom in the midst of their trials. According to verse 5, what can we count on from God when we ask him for wisdom?

✦ Faith is vital to prayer, James says. Doubt, on the other hand, hinders prayer. In verse 6, how does James describe someone who doubts?

✦ Doubters don't receive answers to their prayers, James says in verse 7, and the reason why becomes clear in verse 8. What do we learn about these doubters in verse 8?

> *"Doubters must be willing to leave their questions*
> *behind and trust God with a whole heart."*[4]

It's important to clarify what James means here. The sort of doubt he has in view isn't the questioning of our faith that most of us experience at one time or another. Doubts about creation or the power of the gospel or even about the existence of God himself can assail even the most committed believers on occasion. The kind of doubt James has in mind here ties back to what he's been saying about wisdom and trials—if someone is skeptical that God can or will bring good out of difficulties, how can her heart be open to receive God's goodness when it comes? Or how can she receive wisdom from God if she isn't sure it's actually wise? We can't receive what we don't even believe.

James is the only New Testament writer to use the term *double-minded*, which he does here in verse 8 (and, as we'll see, again later in 4:8). The literal meaning of the Greek word he used is "two-souled." A double-minded person is someone torn between trusting God and wanting to hedge her bets and trust in her own solutions to her problems, or find worldly ways of coping, which leaves her unstable.

3. FADE OR FLOURISH (1:9–11)

In the middle of his teaching about hardships James inserts some instructions about personal wealth. Finding these comments here might seem odd, like James is getting off point, but they actually tie right in with what he's saying about hardships because both poverty and wealth breed difficulties of various kinds. So, rich or poor, the gospel is the only hope for anyone, and it's all that will matter in the long run.

✦ What do the following passages add to your understanding of what James is teaching here in verses 9–11?

· Proverbs 30:7–9

· Matthew 6:24–30

· 1 Timothy 6:6–10

· Hebrews 13:5

4. TEMPTED AND TRIED (1:12–18)

James reminds us in verse 12 that the trials we experience are actually tests that God uses to build our faith. At the beginning of his teaching on trials, James told us to "count it all joy" when trials come because "the testing" of our faith works to perfect our character (vv. 2–3). This perfecting, or maturing, is God's intention in every difficulty we experience. It's why he allows trials into our lives, and it's the work of a loving Father. James writes in this section that those who persevere receive "the crown of life" (v. 12). The crown James most likely has in mind is a laurel wreath, which, back in his day, was placed on the head of victorious athletes.

> *"We are not competing for a small pile of crowns that God will distribute to super-Christians on the last day. No, Jesus wore a crown of thorns so that all who believe would receive the crown of life."*[5]

✦ We might find it hard to understand how a loving God could test his people. What more do we learn about God's purposes for testing from the following passages?

· Genesis 22:1–14

· Deuteronomy 8:2–3

· 1 Peter 4:12–13

The difficulties that the Lord uses to test his people can also become sources of temptation, which is why James goes straight from tests to temptations in this section.

✦ What do we learn from verse 13 about the part God plays in our temptations?

✦ According to verses 14–15, how does temptation progress to outright acts of sin?

....

....

✦ James says that when sin is allowed to grow and grow, eventually it causes death. How do Romans 5:12 and 6:23 clarify what he means?

....

....

....

....

✦ The primary way we can stop temptation cold is with a right understanding of God's ways with us, which James emphasizes here in verses 16–18. He begins with a warning: "Do not be deceived." As you consider what James writes about God's ways in verses 16–18 in the middle of his teaching about tests and temptations, what *deceit* do you think he is warning us about?

....

....

....

....

James calls God the "Father of lights" in verse 17, which points us back to God's creation of stars and sunshine. These lights are a prime example of the kind of gifts God gives to his people.

✦ James says that God's gifts are "good" and "perfect," which includes even the trials he allows into our lives. How does Romans 8:28–39 deepen our understanding of this truth?

....

....

....

....

"Our response to trials reveals our heart condition."[6]

✦ Verse 18 is one of the most important verses in the entire letter of James because it proclaims how believers are born again and where they stand as a result. Our security in this standing must anchor us as we take in all the instructions James is going to give us through the rest of the letter. How does verse 18 show why we are secure in our salvation?

LET'S TALK

1. "Count it all joy" (v. 2), James says about the trials that come into our lives. Truth be told, it takes practice, right? As we go through various difficulties and lean on the Lord to get us through, and then experience the spiritual growth that results, rejoicing comes more easily. Describe a time when your faith was tested. What help did the Lord send, and how did it help bring you through? How were you changed as a result of the trial?

2. James lays out the way temptation progresses toward sin. Identify some practical ways to stop temptation from progressing. Make it personal. How can you stop a particular temptation before it "gives birth" to sin (v. 15)?

WEEK 2

MIRROR, MIRROR ON THE WALL

JAMES 1:19-27

Do you look in the mirror when you first get up, or do you wait until after that first cup of coffee? Some of us do both. There's that first quick glance that assures us nothing went too terribly wrong during the night—no strange new lumps, bumps, or clumps. Then there's that longer, deeper look when we're getting ourselves together for the day—the close-up, well-lit squint so the eyeliner isn't drawn on in a wonky squiggle. The real question is, how long do those reflections linger in your mind? James says it's natural to look in a mirror but then to walk away and simply forget what we've seen there. (I want to be a lot more like that, don't you?) Even so, James's point isn't about an overfocus on our face. For James, a mirror is a metaphor for God's word, which reflects our heart. Sometimes we can think we're in pretty good spiritual shape because we go to church and do studies like these and refrain from gossiping about our neighbors. We tend to compare ourselves to others and think we look pretty good from a spiritual standpoint. But the mirror of God's word might reveal something altogether different. The Bible exposes us—the real us (to see just how deep the exposure goes, take a look at Hebrews 4:12). James doesn't want us to walk away from the word the way we would from a mirror. That's because what the Bible reflects is a lot more important than a piece of glass. God's word not only exposes us to ourselves; it's intended to transform us into the image of our Savior Jesus.

1. TAKE IT IN! (1:19–21)

In this section, verses 19–21, James explains how Christians receive, or take in, God's word—the good news of salvation in Jesus Christ and all God's ways revealed to us in the Bible.

✦ What three things does James tell us to do in verse 19?

1. ....

2. ....

3. ....

✦ What do we learn about anger in verse 20?

....

....

....

....

*"The saving work of the word extends far beyond
the day of salvation. . . . The word of God empowers
daily growth as we travel the road of salvation."*[7]

✦ Study the following proverbs to deepen your understanding of James's words in verses 19–20 and then write a summary statement in the space provided.

· Proverbs 10:19

....

....

....

· Proverbs 14:29

· Proverbs 15:18

· Proverbs 16:32

· Proverbs 17:27

· Proverbs 19:11

✝ Being quick to hear, slow to speak, and slow to anger is vital because:

Verse 21 begins with the word *therefore* or *so*:

> *Therefore* put away all filthiness and rampant wickedness and receive with meekness the implanted word, which is able to save your souls.

Whenever we find this word in the Bible, we need to ask, What is the *therefore* there for? In this case, James is likely linking back to verse 18, where he said that God "brought us forth by the word of truth, that we should be a kind of firstfruits of his creatures." So here's the link: we have been born again by God's word, the gospel; *therefore* we ought to live by that word.

✦ What two things does James tell us to do in verse 21?

1. ....

2. ....

James wants his readers to picture wickedness as dirty clothes that must be stripped off in order to put on something pure and clean. He's not saying that we save ourselves by cleaning up our spiritual act. We simply can't do that! He's saying that putting off sinful ways exposes us to the influence of the gospel that's been planted within our hearts and thereby transforms the way we live. This is the implanted word, James says, that saves souls and works salvation for God's people in the past, the present, and the future.

> *"When we receive 'the implanted word,' we receive freedom from sin and for righteousness. The word is not fundamentally a list of things we can and cannot do. Instead, it is a message from heaven that gives us the joy of being able to live out our theology. We get to be the 'doers,' not the 'don't-doers.' Thus, the more we receive and obey the Word, the more free we become."[8]*

✤ How does Jeremiah 31:33–34 reveal what James means when he describes the word as "implanted"?

_____

_____

_____

_____

✤ According to verse 21, what frame of heart is necessary for the word to penetrate our hearts?

_____

_____

_____

_____

> *"The **meek** are the 'gentle' . . . those who do not assert themselves over others in order to further their own agendas in their own strength."*[9]

2. IT MATTERS WHERE WE LOOK (1:22-25)

In these next few verses, James builds on his teaching about God's word. The Lord implants the word in us, but that's just the beginning. Afterward, we have a part to play as well.

✤ James has been writing about God's word since verse 18 (the last verse of last week's lesson). List all the ways in which James refers to the word in verses 18–25.

1. _____

2. _____

3. _____

4. ....

5. ....

✦ According to verse 22, what is true of those who don't do the word but merely hear it?

....

....

....

....

✦ You've most likely looked at your face in a mirror sometime during the past several hours. Think about why you looked and what you did in response to what you saw. As you reflect on that, how does it explain James's use of this mirror illustration in verses 23–24?

....

....

....

....

Next James contrasts the quick glance of the mirror-looker with someone who studies the word—"the perfect law"—and acts on what he sees there.

✦ James calls the word "the law of liberty" in verse 25. In the Old Testament, the law was holy and good, but it didn't free people. How does Romans 8:1–11 show us why James calls the word "the law of liberty"?

....

....

....

....

✦ James commends a "doer who acts" on what she finds in the word. How exactly do we do what he says here in verse 25? Hint: look back at verse 21. And take time to read Ephesians 4:17–24.

✦ James makes a promise at the end of verse 25: doers of the word will be blessed in their doing. How does Psalm 1:1–3 reveal what this blessing is?

3. TRUE RELIGION (1:26–27)

What makes someone religious? That's where James takes us now, as he continues his instructions about living out the word.

✦ As you look at all James says in verses 26–27, what would you say is the primary difference between pure religion and worthless religion?

God has always required his people to care for the vulnerable in society. Old Testament law mandated that widows, orphans, and the poverty-stricken were to be helped in practical, tangible ways. The requirement is the same for God's people in the New Testament, as we see here in James.

True disciples also keep a careful watch on how they relate to "the world" (v. 27). In the Bible, this term is used for a pursuit of fleshly gratification—getting all we can out of what this world has to offer—and a rejection of God's ways. Read 1 John 2:15–17. What does this passage help us understand about how to keep ourselves "unstained from the world"?

LET'S TALK

1. Describe how God's "implanted word" (v. 21) has changed you, or is still slowly but surely changing you, in an area of sin or personal struggle. Consider especially the three marks of "religion that is pure and undefiled" in verse 27: (1) guarding our tongue, (2) caring for the poor and marginalized, and (3) avoiding worldly influence. How has being united to Christ and indwelt by the Holy Spirit made a tangible difference in how you live? And where you see failure, which particular verses in James 1 provide you comfort, hope, and encouragement?

2. James warns against giving way to a quick temper, because, he says, anger "does not produce the righteousness of God" (vv. 19–20). Given that it doesn't produce God's righteousness, what does it produce instead? If you struggle with anger, explain how you can apply, in a practical, real way, James's proposed remedy in verse 21.

PLAYING FAVORITES

JAMES 2:1-13

Many of us remember the teen angst of not quite fitting in, or, if we did fit in, how we applied ourselves meticulously to retain that in-crowd status. Our hairstyle and our clothes were carefully chosen with an eye to gaining the approval of those with whom we wanted to be identified. Truth be told, the craving doesn't vanish after high school; grown-up girls—in other words, women—just become a bit more sophisticated in how they pursue it. Some of us feel desperate to belong, even in places where belonging is determined by clothing, career, address, and bank account. It's human default, after all. But it's a worldly default, and as Christians we are called to reject this sort of evaluation both for ourselves and for others. So do we? It's worth thinking about. Maybe we're just a little bit more friendly to people whose invitations we crave. Or perhaps we show just a tad more interest in people who can benefit our lives or the lives of our loved ones in some material way. James brings this issue front and center in this week's study, showing us that even redeemed believers can fall into the sin of partiality—of playing favorites.

1. CHRISTIANS CAN'T BE KISS-UPS (2:1-4)

James paints a picture of two very different men who walk into a gathering, most likely an assembly of church members. The first man is obviously wealthy, while the second is clearly poor. The issue here is how each of the two is treated.

✦ What clear instruction does James give in verse 1 for people who gather together as they seek to live by faith?

....

....

....

....

✦ James says that using wealth as a factor in determining how to treat people springs from evil thoughts (v. 4). Why do you think James classifies such thinking as outright evil?

....

....

....

....

✦ What do you think underlies the temptation to cater to the wealthy in particular?

....

....

....

....

2. UPSIDE-DOWN THINKING (2:5–7)

"Listen," James urges as he begins verse 5. It seems he wants us to pay careful attention to what he's about to write. He wants his readers not only to take in his words but to do some self-examination in the process.

✦ James reminds us in verse 5 that God's choice of people to elevate is very different from the choices we naturally make: "Has not God chosen those who are poor in the world to be rich in faith and heirs of the kingdom?" (v. 5). How does 1 Corinthians 1:27–28 help us make sense of why God chooses as he does?

....

....

....

....

✣ Believers reading James's letter back in his day would have been at very least un-comfortable, if not downright ashamed, when they read what James says about the rich in verse 6. What foolishness does he call out here?

....

....

....

....

In every age, wealth and at least a measure of power typically go hand in hand. In James's day, some rich people used their money to manipulate the legal system to take away even the little that the poor had. These wealthy folks could charge high interest rates and impose unrealistic fines for late payments, then use the courts to force the poor off their very own land.[10]

✣ That's why James reminds them, "Are not the rich the ones who oppress you, and the ones who drag you into court?" (v. 6). But James's reminder goes beyond the mistreatment of his readers. Underlying all his counsel here is concern for what pleases the Lord. What does Leviticus 25:35–38 reveal about God's will when it comes to wealth disparity?

....

....

....

....

James asks one more reminder question about wealthy oppressors in verse 7: "Are they not the ones who blaspheme the honorable name by which you were called?" To *blaspheme* is to slander God and say terrible, untrue things about his character or about his people. We don't know the specific situation James had in mind here. He might have had in mind unbelievers mocking God or the gospel of Jesus Christ or people making fun of Christians seeking to live as disciples of Jesus.

> ### Rich and Poor in James's Day
>
> "A small group of wealthy landowners and merchants accumulated more and more power, while large numbers of people were forced from their land and grew even poorer. Most of James's readers probably belonged to this class of poor agricultural laborers."[11]

3. LIVING THE ROYAL LAW (2:8–13)

Still on the topic of favoritism, James makes clear that favoring the rich over the poor isn't just shallow and unkind—it violates God's law, which makes it downright sinful.

✤ James refers to the "royal law" in verse 8. How do the following passages explain why James calls it "royal"? Be sure to note what is distinctive in each passage.

- Matthew 22:36–40

....

....

....

- Romans 13:8–10

....

....

....

· Galatians 5:13–15

....

....

....

· James calls the law "royal" because:

....

....

....

✦ Just like believers in James's day, we need to guard against misunderstanding what it means to obey God's law. A common misunderstanding is to look at our obedience as if it were a balance sheet, and so long as our obedience column is longer than our disobedience column, we're doing okay. How does James correct that wrong thinking in verses 8–10?

....

....

....

....

In verse 11 James uses two of the Ten Commandments to illustrate his point: don't be unfaithful to your spouse and don't murder. (To view all ten commandments as they were given by God to Moses, see Exodus 20:1–17.) It's likely James chose these two commandments because they epitomize what it means to love and not harm our neighbor.

Bible Study Principle:
Let Scripture interpret Scripture.

We saw that James refers to the "royal law" in verse 8. Now in verse 12, he brings in the "law of liberty," or the law that gives freedom. (He did the same thing back in 1:25, and we looked at Romans 8:1–11 to understand what he meant by "law of liberty.") James instructs us to keep in mind, as we live our lives, that we are going be judged under this law of liberty. His point is that our security in Christ doesn't free us from the need to obey God—it just sets obedience "on a new footing. No longer is God's law a threatening, confining burden. For the will of God now confronts us . . . an obligation we discharge in the joyful knowledge that God has both 'liberated' us from the penalty of sin and given us, in his Spirit, the power to obey his will."[12]

When James cautions his readers to live their lives aware of final judgment, we have to keep in mind that his words are addressed to believers, those who belong to Christ Jesus by faith. James's words might at first seem to contradict what we find elsewhere in the Bible, such as what Jesus said: "Truly, truly, I say to you, whoever hears my word and believes him who sent me has eternal life. He does not come into judgment, but has passed from death to life" (John 5:24). But since there is nothing contradictory in God's word, our job is to figure out how to interpret James's words in light of what Jesus said. In other words, we must allow Scripture to interpret Scripture.

✦ So as we consider what James writes about facing judgment alongside what Jesus said about Christians *not* facing it, how can we best understand what James is saying in verse 12? (A look at 1 Corinthians 3:11–15 will help you answer.)

....

....

....

....

James brings the importance of mercy into his teaching about judgment. "Judgment is without mercy to one who has shown no mercy," he writes in verse 13. He likely has in mind the "law of retribution"—an eye for an eye—but, more importantly, the words of Jesus: "Whatever you wish that others would do to you, do also to them, for this is the Law and the Prophets" (Matthew 7:12). Those words of Jesus's are traditionally called the "Golden Rule." James's overarching point here isn't that our failure to show mercy disqualifies us from salvation. Rather, when we do show mercy to others, it is evidence that we *are* truly saved.

✦ What do the following passages teach us about how to show mercy to others?

   · Zechariah 7:9–10

   · Matthew 18:23–33

A glimpse of the gospel ends this section: "Mercy triumphs over judgment" (v. 13). For those in Christ, mercy always has the last word. Yes, showing mercy to others gives evidence of our union with Christ. But in this lifetime, we are never going to do it perfectly or even adequately. What matters is whether the bent of our hearts and lives—and words and deeds—are directed toward others in compassion and kindness.

LET'S TALK

1. What criteria do we use for deciding which friendships to invest in? Conversely, how much of ourselves do we invest in those who can't benefit us in any way?

....

....

2. We can't help but be convicted of sin by this week's lesson, which is why James's reminder that God's mercy triumphs over judgment (v. 13) comes at the perfect time. And not only are we recipients of God's mercy through our union with Christ; we also live now under the "law of liberty" (v. 12), which means we are no longer helpless in the fight against sin and the sinful habits that try to ensnare us. Even so, who among us hasn't failed to love our neighbor this week (this day, this hour)? The question isn't whether we sin; it's how we respond to it after we do. How can the fact of our standing with God—the fact that we are covered by his mercy and counted righteous in his eyes—reshape how we wage war against our sin?

BEWARE OF FAKE FAITH

JAMES 2:14-26

"Not everyone who says to me, 'Lord, Lord,' will enter the kingdom of heaven, but the one who does the will of my Father who is in heaven," Jesus said, in some of the most sobering words he ever uttered. He was warning people about faith that isn't real. It looks real, it sounds real, but it's fake faith. Among these faith-fakers are good, church-goers who raise successful children and don't cheat on their spouse. Also included are people who know the Bible and can even teach it and carry out ministries in the name of Jesus. They simply drift through life expecting that their upstanding morals and ministries impress God and will secure their salvation. But their heart isn't in it, or, better said, their heart is in it for themselves, not for the Lord. What's so scary is that they refuse to look at reality until it's too late. Then when they discover that they're shut out of heaven, they express dismay and plead their case, but the Lord replies, "I never knew you; depart from me, you workers of lawlessness" (Matthew 7:21–23). James has a similar warning in this week's lesson, and we can't help but want to examine our hearts as we study. James and Jesus come at the problem from different angles. Where Jesus calls out works with no faith, James calls out faith with no works, but both Jesus and James are getting at the same thing—make sure your faith is the real thing! How can we tell? James is going to show us.

1. FAKE FAITH (2:14-17)

James stretches his readers' minds in this section. He wants them—and us—to think, and he stimulates our thoughts with a couple of questions.

James asks, "What good is it, my brothers [and sisters], if someone says he has faith but does not have works? Can that faith save him?" (v. 14). Wait a minute—doesn't the rest of the New Testament teach that works can't save anyone? James seems to be contradicting that teaching, but we know that nothing in the Bible is contradictory. Every word is true. Our task is to see how all these various teachings fit together—to allow the Bible to interpret itself.

✦ With that Bible study principle in mind—allowing the Bible to interpret itself—how does Ephesians 2:8–10 shed light on what James means here in verse 14 about the connection between good works and salvation?

Both the apostle Paul, who wrote Ephesians, and James link faith and good works, and even though Paul and James seem to contradict each other, they are actually teaching the same principle—good works are the *result* of salvation by faith, not the cause of it. And both Paul and James agree about faith too: faith doesn't save us—only Christ does. Faith is merely the means—the instrument—of salvation.

It's vitally important that we understand not only what James is saying here in verse 14 but also what he *isn't* saying:

- He is *not* saying that good works save.
- He is *not* saying that faith itself saves.
- He *is* saying that genuine faith inevitably produces good works.

✦ In verses 15–16, James illustrates his point with an example that ties in with what he wrote about earlier—the godly way to treat disadvantaged people. What point is James making in this illustration?

✝ In verse 17 James summarizes the point he's been making in verses 14–16. Rewrite his summary statement in your own words.

2. WHEN BELIEF ISN'T ENOUGH (2:18-19)

The point James is making about faith and works is so vitally important that he sets up an argument with an imaginary critic to reinforce his lesson.

✝ What does James's imaginary critic argue in verse 18, and how does James respond in that same verse? (Try to answer using your own words.)

In verse 19 James commends his imaginary critic for believing that "God is one." James gets this *oneness* of God from a sermon Moses preached to Israel centuries before. During that sermon Moses said, "Hear, O Israel: The Lord our God, the Lord is one" (Deuteronomy 6:4). He was proclaiming that the Lord alone is God—the only God.

✝ The imaginary critic isn't the only one who believes in the "oneness" of God. James tells us that demons believe it too, even though they are evil beings. What does this tell us about the nature of this belief—the faith of demons and people like James's imaginary critic?

....

....

....

....

....

....

....

....

> ### The Shema
>
> "Hear, O Israel: The Lord our God, the Lord is one" (Deuteronomy 6:4). This verse is called the *Shema* from the Hebrew word for "hear." The Lord alone is Israel's God, "the only one." The statement points to God's exclusivity.

✝ Read Jesus's teaching in Matthew 7:15–20, where he talks about how to identify false teachers. What do Jesus's words there add to your understanding of how faith and works go hand in hand?

....

....

....

....

3. PORTRAITS OF LIVING FAITH (2:20-26)

Still engaging his imaginary critic—in rather harsh terms, calling him a "foolish person" (v. 20)—James strengthens his argument with two Old Testament examples: Abraham and Rahab.

✢ What does James say in verse 20 about faith that's unaccompanied by works?

....

....

....

....

✢ James turns our attention to an important event in the life of Abraham, the patriarch from whom God's people, Israel, descended. Before we look at this event though, we need to go back a bit earlier in Abraham's life. Read Genesis 15:1–6. Why does the Lord count Abraham as righteous?

....

....

....

....

So God came and promised Abraham a son, but Abraham was made to wait years for the fulfillment of this promise. Then, in God's perfect time, a son, Isaac, was born to Abraham and his wife Sarah. A few years later, something significant happened. Take a few minutes to read about it in Genesis 22:1–14.

✢ What does James say in 2:21–22 about Abraham's faith during this event?

....

....

....

....

✢ In 2:23–24, James goes back to that earlier episode in Abraham's life—the time when God promised him galaxies' worth of descendants and Abraham was counted righteous because he believed God—and ties it into this later event, the sacrifice of

Isaac. According to James, how do those two events in Abraham's life link together to establish his faith?

_____

_____

_____

_____

✦ James's second example of true faith is Rahab the prostitute. She comes into the Bible story when God's people Israel, Abraham's descendants, were preparing to enter the promised land. Read her story in Joshua 2:1–21; 6:15–25 and Hebrews 11:31. What specifically did Rahab do and say that confirmed the genuineness of her faith?

_____

_____

_____

_____

In the centuries since the New Testament was written, some people have been troubled by the language James uses when he says that Abraham and Rahab were *"justified by works"* (2:21 and 2:25). They think that James's teaching here contradicts the teaching of the great apostle Paul, who wrote: "We hold that one is *justified by faith* apart from works of the law" (Romans 3:28). But as we noted earlier, nothing in God's word is contradictory. So the best way to understand James's words is to hold them up side by side with Paul's words. As we do, we realize that James's words complement rather than contradict Paul's words. We can be confident of this, because what came from the pen of two men—James and Paul—is actually part of the single, unified word from the one true God. So when James writes that "a person is justified by works and not by faith alone" (2:24), he's talking about people who have head knowledge of the Lord that never penetrates their heart so that they act on it—fake faith. Paul's point is that faith, not good deeds, is the instrument through which God saves us. So James and Paul are really just using the word "justified" in slightly different ways, and both argue that true faith always produces righteous works.

God's Word	
James's words:	Paul's words:
"You see that a person is justified by works and not by faith alone." (James 2:24)	"For we hold that one is justified by faith apart from works of the law." (Romans 3:28)
Justified = verified, proved	Justified = declared righteous
Good works are evidence of salvation	Good works do not produce salvation

LET'S TALK

1. How has your faith been evidenced in words and deeds? In other words, how has your faith brought about concrete change in your life—change that is made manifest in specific deeds? Conversely, where might you be tempted to equate good deeds or success in a ministry activity with mature faith? Talk about how we can know when our deeds spring from our faith or from some other motivation.

2. Both Abraham and Rahab took great risks because of their faith. Abraham risked the loss of his precious son; Rahab risked the loss of her life. Describe a time when your faith led you to make a costly sacrifice. What was the outcome, both in your life and in your walk with the Lord?

SALT POND OR FRESH WATER?

JAMES 3:1-12

"You're funny-looking"—that playground taunt. "You'll never amount to anything"—the outpouring of a frustrated, angry mother. The playground bully and upset mom might soon forget what they said, but recipients of those words are likely to remember. Maybe always. The most painful of these memories come from manipulative, abusive words designed to subdue another for selfish, evil purposes. Whatever their origin, words once spoken can't be unsaid or covered over with new, better words or blotted out by time. Kind, encouraging, cruel, or careless words matter. And what we say reveals who we are—not only the actual words we use but the way in which we use them. Early in his letter James said that the way someone talks is an indicator of her heart and determines the impact of her walk with the Lord: "If anyone thinks he is religious and does not bridle his tongue but deceives his heart, this person's religion is worthless" (1:26). Do we use our words to build up or tear down, to love or to hate, to help or to hurt? Yes, our tongue has that much power. In fact, our words have so much power that James devotes an entire section of his letter—the twelve verses we're studying this week—to the power of our words.

1. SMALL SIZE, BIG BOASTS (3:1-5)

Words have consequences. That's what James wants us to see as he dives deep into the topic of the tongue.

In verse 1 James gives a warning to people who want to become teachers (he has in mind particularly teachers of God's word). At first glance, his warning might seem misplaced here—how does it fit into this section, which is all about the tongue? But it actually fits quite nicely. James singles out teachers because, in the process of teaching, they must utter a lot of words! And the more words one says, the greater the risk of sinful slips of the tongue.

✦ Teachers of biblical truth have tremendous influence over those they teach—an additional reason for James's special caution in verse 1. How do the following passages reveal the sort of influence that Bible teachers are meant to have and thus why their words matter so much?

· 2 Timothy 2:1–2

· 2 Timothy 2:24

· Titus 2:1–3

"Spiritual maturity is evidenced by the use of the tongue. The mastery of it is one of the clearest marks of a whole person, a true Christian. Tongue-mastery is the fruit of self-mastery."[13]

✦ If only we could control our tongues, we'd be able to achieve perfection, James says in verse 2. How does James use horses and ships to show us why such an achievement is out of our reach?

✦ What specific tongue sin does James name in verse 5, and how would you define that sin?

✦ What does Psalm 12:3–4 reveal about what underlies the nature of the tongue sin named in verse 5?

✦ How does the fire imagery James uses in verse 5 show the extent of the damage the tongue can cause?

2. TONGUES ON FIRE (3:6-8)

James paints more pictures of the power of the human tongue.

✦ James says that the tongue is "set on fire by hell" (v. 6). How does each of the following passages illuminate what he means?

· Genesis 3:1–4

· John 8:44

· Revelation 12:7–9

> "Word problems are not vocabulary problems. Word
> problems are not technique problems. Word problems
> in their essential form are heart problems."[14]

✦ How does the contrast James sets up in verses 7 and 8 show us our need for the Savior?

....

....

🌱 James describes the tongue as "a restless evil, full of deadly poison" (v. 8). From the proverbs in the chart that follows, identify the specific tongue sins and where those sins lead.

	Tongue "Poison"	Consequence
Proverbs 7:21-23		
Proverbs 15:4		
Proverbs 16:28		
Proverbs 17:20		
Proverbs 18:6		
Proverbs 19:5		
Proverbs 26:28		

3. DOUBLE TALK (3:9-12)

So far we've seen that the tongue has tremendous power and, because of that power, what we say can be deadly. Now James uncovers another reality—double talk.

🌱 James describes double talk in verses 9 and 10. How would you summarize what he says about it?

....

....

✦ Look at James's illustrations of a spring and a fig tree in verses 11–12. What point is James making in these verses?

> *"Our only hope as we pursue the discipline of self that leads to mastery of the tongue is that we are Christ's and that we are being made increasingly like him. . . . Do you speak like someone who 'sounds' a little like Jesus because, born broken in your consciousness of your sinful tongue, you have found pardon and renewal in Christ, and now his Word dwells richly in you? At the end of the day, that is what spiritual maturity looks like—or better, sounds like— because of the transformation of our use of the tongue."*[15]

✦ Before James, Jesus taught about the tongue, and he placed a lot of weight on the words people say. Read Jesus's teaching in Matthew 12:33–37 and 15:18–19. What reality does Jesus reveal in these passages?

> *"Bad things don't produce good things.*
> *And so a person who is not right with God*
> *and walking daily in his presence cannot*
> *consistently speak pure and helpful words.*
> *One who is double and inconsistent with*
> *regard to the things of God in his heart . . . will*
> *be double and inconsistent in his speech."*[16]

LET'S TALK

1. James says the tongue is "full of deadly poison" (v. 8). Describe a time you experienced the truth of that description, either in words you heard or in words you said. What was the long-term impact?

2. In what specific ways do you find yourself most prone to sin with your tongue? You might want to glance back at the proverbs chart on page 59. Consider why this area might be such a struggle for you.

....

....

....

....

....

....

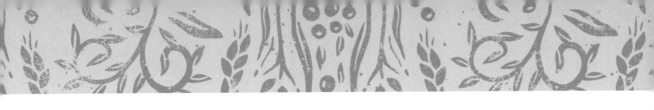

WISDOM OF THE WORLD OR WISDOM OF THE WORD

JAMES 3:13-18

"Love yourself first and everything else falls into line. You really have to love yourself to get anything done in this world," Lucille Ball reportedly once said.[17] Many, perhaps the majority, of those who heard her surely nodded in agreement, assessing her words as wisdom because, after all, the merit of one's words can be measured by success, right? And not many have had more success than Lucille Ball. But if her words are truly wise—love yourself first and everything else falls into line—that would mean Jesus was an utter failure, because he gave his life for others. But the Bible tells us just the opposite. Jesus was the wisest man who ever lived (1 Corinthians 1:23–25). So it seems there are two types of wisdom for us to choose from. One is the "love yourself first" kind, which is driven by envy and self-serving ambition—the wisdom of the *world*. The other kind of wisdom lives for the Lord and for serving others—the wisdom of the *word*. At all times, in every choice and activity and relationship, we must choose either the wisdom of the world or the wisdom of the word. This week James shows us how to discern between the two types of wisdom and also how to define our lives by the only type that is truly wise.

1. WISE WORKS (3:13)

James loves to ask questions, the kind that make us think, and that's exactly how he begins this new section on wisdom. Are we wise and understanding women? James wants us to do some self-examination along these lines.

✦ According to verse 13, how do we know whether we can consider ourselves wise?

_____

_____

_____

_____

_____

_____

_____

✦ What do you think James means in verse 13 by "good conduct"?

_____

_____

_____

_____

_____

Meekness

Meekness, or gentleness, was considered a sign of weakness in the days of the early church, but Jesus elevated it to a primary Christian virtue (Matthew 5:5; 11:29). Genuine meekness has no root in cowardice or passivity. It springs from trusting God and therefore being set free from anxious self-promotion.[18]

James identifies a trait of wisdom—meekness. He calls it "the meekness of wisdom" (v. 13). The word "meekness" comes from a Greek word that can also be translated as "gentleness." In the culture of James's day, meekness, or gentleness, meant weakness. It was not a virtue in the eyes of the world.

✦ Read Philippians 2:3–11, where we see the meekness of Jesus, and answer the following questions.

· How in this Philippians passage does Jesus demonstrate that meekness is actually strength rather than weakness?

· What characteristics of meekness are revealed in Philippians 2:3–11?

2. WORTHLESS WISDOM (3:14–16)

There's another type of wisdom, an ungodly wisdom, that stands in stark contrast to the wisdom that's characterized by meekness, and that's where James takes us next.

✦ James makes clear what produces ungodly wisdom. What sources of ungodly wisdom does James identify in verses 14 and 15?

James calls us to do some soul searching in these verses. In verse 16 he tells us that the wrong kind of wisdom produces disorder. As we consider our lives—at home, at work, and in our relationships—do we generally find order and peace, or is there more often friction and chaos? Wherever chaos has gotten the upper hand so that it dominates, the first place to look for answers is our own heart. Is jealousy or ambition ruling us? We want to be sure to note that James is careful to identify the type of jealousy and ambition that leads us into trouble—*bitter* jealousy and *selfish* ambition. It's an important distinction, because there is good jealousy and good ambition.

✦ How do the following passages enable us to understand the difference between godly jealousy and ambition and the kind that leads to chaos?

Jealousy and Ambition	
	Portrayals of Jealousy
Exodus 20:5-6	
Numbers 25:10-13	
Song of Solomon 8:6-7	
Romans 11:13-14	
2 Corinthians 11:2	

Jealousy and Ambition	
	Portrayals of Ambition
Ezekiel 33:30–31	
2 Corinthians 5:8–9	
2 Corinthians 13:11	
Philippians 1:15–17	
1 Timothy 3:1	

> "*God demands the fidelity of his people because he loves them, but ultimately because he is most glorified when they ascribe to him the honor that belongs to him alone. . . . Only God deserves absolute honor, worship, and glory, and he reacts with jealousy and anger when those he has created do not ascribe it to him, or when they desire it for themselves. When God's people deeply desire that he be glorified so that nothing competes with him for our devotion and worship, they should experience a godly jealousy that mirrors his.*"[19]

Godly jealousy is protective. It's the sort of jealousy the Lord feels when his people turn away from him to worship idols, or the jealousy a husband feels when his marriage is threatened. Bitter jealousy, on the other hand, wants to take away, not protect. It's characterized by greed and envy. Wisdom that's characterized by bitter jealousy is the polar opposite of godly wisdom, the kind that is marked by humility, or meekness, and it's a flat-out denial of true, godly wisdom. And it leads to boasting, James says, which has to do with placing confidence in the wrong things.

3. WISDOM FROM ABOVE (3:17–18)

Godly wisdom is the only real wisdom, and that's where James takes us next with a beautiful description.

✦ Godly wisdom is much to be desired, of course, but left to ourselves, we'd never attain it. That's because, James says, this wisdom is "from above" (v. 17). How does each of the following passages illuminate why James calls it "wisdom from above"?

　· Romans 16:25–27

· 1 Corinthians 1:26–31

· Ephesians 1:16–17

✢ James lists the traits of godly wisdom in verse 17. How might each trait play out in a real-life situation or relationship? Provide examples from your own life. A related word or two has been provided.

· Wisdom from above is *pure* (innocent, holy):

· Wisdom from above is *peaceable* (yielding, promotes well-being):

· Wisdom from above is *gentle* (considerate):

· Wisdom from above is *open to reason* (humble, open-minded):

· Wisdom from above is *full of mercy and good fruits* (godliness in action):

· Wisdom from above is *impartial* (straightforward, undivided):

· Wisdom from above is *sincere* (stable, trustworthy, transparent):

✦ What overarching trait of godly wisdom does James name in verse 18, and what does it produce?

LET'S TALK

1. Identify some sources of worldly wisdom. Which ones have tempted you or drawn you in, and why did they appeal? What enabled you to eventually see them as the wrong kind of wisdom?

2. How can we determine whether something we are pursuing or doing is being driven by bitter jealousy and selfish ambition or by protective jealousy and godly ambition?

ALL OR NOTHING

JAMES 4:1-12

A loving husband doted on his bride, lavishing her with good gifts and the provision of all her needs. He delighted in her companionship and her trust, and he made sure she was safe at all times, protected under his watchful eye and in his strength. As far as husbands go, he was everything a bride could possibly want. Yet she betrayed him. She was ungrateful and arrogant, which made her dissatisfied with all he was for her, so she went looking for other lovers to fulfill her cravings. He knew of her adultery, of course. But he didn't kick her out. Instead he did all he could to win her back, and he waited. She eventually did come back, but not for long. She cheated on him again. And again. His love never grew cold, even while his jealousy burned hot. To this day he loves his bride and will never forsake her. The story reads like the script from a Lifetime TV movie, doesn't it? But the Old Testament prophets are the ones who tell the story of God the betrayed husband and Israel, his faithless bride. (If you want a glimpse of the backstory, read Jeremiah 2:2–8, 31–32 and Hosea 1–3.) In the passage we'll study this week, James no doubt had this imagery in mind when he calls out the adultery of those reading his letter. The believers to whom he writes were forming an illicit friendship with the world, and therefore they were betraying their exclusive relationship with the Lord. In this week's lesson, James shines light on what happens as a result of spiritual adultery, the impact it has on our hearts and the trouble it breeds in all our relationships. And then he shows God's straying people how to return to their heavenly bridegroom.

1. PASSIONS AT WAR (4:1-3)

It's the rare day we don't witness a disagreement of some sort, from children's squabbles to Twitter wars. Sadly, quarrels and fights are so commonplace that we become numb to hostile words, bitter tears, and angry silences. It happens everywhere, in businesses, in schools, and in families—and even in the church, among God's people.

✦ James says in verse 1 that quarrels arise because "your passions are at war within you" (v. 1). How does he explain these warring passions in verse 2?

....

....

....

✦ What reasons does James give in this opening section for why these contentious believers don't have what they desire—and even what they request from God?

1. ....

....

2. ....

....

✦ James speaks directly to motives here, to what underlies our desires. Our motives, in turn, affect not only how we pray but how God answers our prayers. How do the following passages show this more thoroughly?

· Psalm 37:4

....

....

....

· Matthew 7:7–11

....

....

....

· 1 John 5:14

2. ADULTERERS! (4:4–5)

As we noted at the beginning of the week, God's relationship with his people is sometimes pictured as a marriage. He safeguards this exclusive bond with protective love and zeal. We see glimpses of that imagery here in verses 4–5.

✦ Before we take a close look at verses 4–5, let's look a bit more at how the Lord views his relationship with his people. Read the following passages and then summarize in a sentence or two what strikes you most.

· Isaiah 54:5

· Jeremiah 31:31–33

· Ephesians 5:25–27

· Revelation 19:6–9

· What strikes me most is:

Friendship in James's Day

"James censures adultery, but he even objects to friendship with the world. . . . We use the word 'friend' lightly, when we really mean 'cordial acquaintance.' But in antiquity, as today, true friends shared a mind-set and an outlook on life. They shared interests, values, and goals. They saw life in much the same way. They shared goods as necessary. They cared for each other and worked together effectively because they agreed how the work should be done."[20]

✦ Why does James call the people he is addressing "adulterous"?

✦ Why do you think that a committed Christian cannot be a "friend of the world" (v. 4)? Let 1 John 2:15–16 help guide your answer.

Bible scholars have struggled over the centuries to understand some of what James writes in verse 5. Is "the spirit that he has made to dwell in us" the Holy Spirit? Or is James referring to the human spirit that God put into each human being? Since James doesn't mention the Holy Spirit specifically, it seems best to interpret this spirit as the human spirit. It just fits the context of what he is teaching. Another difficulty is the quote in verse 5: "the Scripture says . . ." But there is no one particular verse in the Bible where we find what James cites in verse 5. So in this case, it seems that James has the whole of God's word in mind, its overall teaching.

✦ What does James reveal about the Lord in verse 5, and how does it tie into the marriage imagery we've detected in this section?

> "They are married to Jesus, but they run after other gods.
> This endangers their relationship, their marriage, to him.
> . . . Just as faithless Israel sought to worship both the
> Lord and the Canaanite gods of fertility and prosperity,
> so Christians attempt to pursue both God and the world.
> James says that this is not vacillation; it is adultery."[21]

3. GRACE, HUMILITY—AND MORE GRACE (4:6-12)

Unfaithful though we are at times, the Lord not only welcomes us but also enables us, with fresh supplies of his grace, to draw near to him. James shows us how.

✦ James begins this section by encouraging us. God doesn't forsake his people, even when they are unfaithful to him. To the contrary, he "gives more grace" (v. 6). But there's a condition attached that influences how we experience this grace. Drawing from Proverbs 3:34, James makes it clear here in verse 6. What is this condition?

....

....

....

....

✦ Read Daniel 4:28–37. What do we learn from what happened to the ancient Babylonian King Nebuchadnezzar about how God "opposes" the proud?

....

....

....

....

✦ What do we learn about humility from the following passages and why the Lord values it in his people?

· Proverbs 22:4

....

....

....

· Micah 6:8

....

....

....

· Ephesians 4:1–3

· Philippians 2:3–8

· 1 Peter 5:6

✦ How, according to James in verse 7, do we go about humbling ourselves?

✦ What do we learn from Ephesians 6:11–18 about how to resist the devil?

> *"To 'humble ourselves before the Lord' means to recognize our own spiritual poverty, to acknowledge consequently our desperate need of God's help, and to submit to his commanding will for our lives."*[22]

✦ James holds out a promise in verse 8: "Draw near to God, and he will draw near to you." What does he add in this verse about *how* we draw near?

....

....

....

....

For the second time in his letter, in verse 8, James uses the term *double-minded*. You can look back at 1:8 to see the first instance. If you recall, a double-minded woman is one who's torn between wanting God and wanting the world.

✦ James commands double-minded people to both wash their hands and purify their hearts. We find those two words, *cleanse* (or *wash*) and *purify*, used together in the Old Testament to describe rituals that priests had to perform when carrying out their duties. But by James's day, all those priestly rituals were no longer necessary. Jesus Christ, by his death on the cross, abolished the need for those Old Testament rituals. So when James calls God's people to take steps to cleanse their hands and purify their hearts, what do you think he means?

....

....

....

....

✦ Continuing his call for a spiritual turnaround, James calls God's people to mourn and weep and to turn their joy into gloom (v. 9). At first glance, his words are anything but encouraging, right? But if we keep the context in mind—the bigger picture of what he's teaching here—we'll see that his words are meant to bring hope, not despair. What overall, in verses 6–10, is James calling God's people to do, and how does this overall call help us understand verse 9? Hint (if you need one): take a look at Joel 2:12 and 2 Corinthians 7:10.

We can view verses 11–12 as basically a summary of everything James has been teaching about how Christians are to treat one another as they live out their faith. He's emphasized the significance of our words, not only how they impact others but in what they convey about the state of our own hearts. Trash-talking is the fruit of arrogant boasting (3:5), jealousy (3:14, 16), self-centered desires (4:1, 3), and pride (4:6).[23] At first glance, it's hard to get why James brings Old Testament law into his argument here, but it makes sense when we realize that he likely has a specific portion of that law in mind—Leviticus 19. There we find a command against slander (19:12), but overarching that, in the very same chapter, is one of the greatest commands of all:

> You shall not take vengeance or bear a grudge against the sons of your own people, but you shall love your neighbor as yourself: I am the LORD. (Leviticus 19:18)

So James seems to be saying that criticizing other believers violates the command to love our neighbor. Plus it's an act of standing in judgment against our Christian brothers and sisters. Added to that, James writes in verse 16, we judge the law when we fail to keep it. The arrogance of sitting in critical judgment against others is like saying God's laws about not slandering and about loving our neighbor don't matter. That's what it means to sit in judgment not only on people but on the very ways of God!

LET'S TALK

1. James shows us that fractured relationships and envy of others is an indicator that we are cheating on the Lord with the world. Consider what else might be an indicator of worldly love in our hearts. In what way or ways do you find yourself tempted to befriend the world at the expense of your relationship with the Lord?

2. Review the steps James outlines in verses 6–10 for drawing near to the Lord. How might one or more of these steps be necessary to apply in your own life right now? Describe what you will do.

ARROGANCE, SELF-DECEPTION, AND THE SOVEREIGNTY OF GOD

JAMES 4:13–17

It's been aptly said that sometimes you don't know God is all you need until God is all you have. When we're feeling self-sufficient, we aren't consciously aware of our absolute dependence on the Lord for every single thing. But our lack of awareness doesn't change the reality—at all times, in every circumstance, self-sufficiency is only an illusion. Our absolute dependence on God can be hard to grasp when our hard work pays off and circumstances go the way we planned. At such times we can lose sight of biblical wisdom, which reminds us that "the heart of man plans his way, but the Lord establishes his steps" (Proverbs 16:9). Yes, sure, we can accomplish all kinds of things, but only because the Lord enables us, and the truth is, our accomplishments have real value only when they are done in and through our walk with him. That's why Jesus said, "Apart from me you can do nothing" (John 15:5). We see from the Bible that the temptation to trust in ourselves, to believe we are self-sufficient, is nothing new in our day. Way back in the time of Moses, before God's people had grown into a great nation, the Lord warned them about the danger of self-sufficiency:

> Beware lest you say in your heart, "My power and the might of my hand have gotten me this wealth." You shall remember the Lord your God, for it is he who gives you power to get wealth. (Deuteronomy 8:17–18)

Can you see it? Our lives aren't up to us. Achieving our goals and reaching our hopes and dreams—whatever they might be in the various parts of our lives—are determined only by God. James brings all this front and center in the portion of his letter that we'll be studying this week. As we'll see, his instructions aren't so much about the particular activities we engage in as about our attitude in the process.

1. THE BEST-LAID PLANS . . . (4:13–14)

"Come now," James begins, as he calls the business people of the church to pay attention to his words (v. 13).

✦ It seems that James, in verses 13–14, is rebuking business people for making plans. But we can know that's not the right way to understand these verses because of what we find on this subject elsewhere in the Bible, including several of the proverbs. What plan-making principle is revealed in each of the proverbs in the "Plan-Making in Proverbs" chart that follows?

Plan-Making in Proverbs	
Proverbs 6:6–8	
Proverbs 16:3	
Proverbs 16:9	
Proverbs 19:21	
Proverbs 20:18	

✦ The Bible indicates that plan-making is wise, so we know James isn't condemning it here when he calls out people who are mapping their career plans. But all is not well with those whom James is addressing. What words do you detect in verse 13 that indicate a problem?

✦ Jesus told a parable about a successful businessman in Luke 12:15–21. What do you see in the parable that sheds more light on the problem here in James 4:13–14?

✦ The apostle Paul made plans—in fact, planning was an absolute necessity before undertaking his three arduous missionary journeys to spread the good news of the gospel. Read Acts 16:6–10, which recounts an episode where Paul's plans abruptly changed. How does Paul's approach to planning stand in contrast to the sort of planning that James describes in verses 13–14?

✦ James says that we are "a mist that appears for a little time and then vanishes" (v. 14). How does Psalm 90 show us how to respond to the rather grim picture that James paints?

"If we think we can dictate *tomorrow through good planning, we may be even more foolish than those who refuse to plan. No one makes plans for God, and no one knows all that he has planned. That we do not know or control what tomorrow brings, though, does not mean we should not give some serious thought to tomorrow. It means we make all our plans with open hands and heads bowed. And we pray that reality will far surpass our plans. How boring would it be if our lives always played out according to our own plans?"*[24]

2. THE REMEDY AND THE HINDRANCE (4:15-16)

James identified the problem in verses 13–14, and now, in verses 15–16, he provides the remedy for the problem as well as what hinders people from embracing that remedy.

✦ According to verse 15, how should we make our plans, whether for business or any other circumstance?

James has sharp words for the people he is addressing in this section: "You boast in your arrogance" (v. 16). It's important to note that boasting in the New Testament isn't necessarily negative. The apostle Paul used the term to indicate a godly confidence (see 2 Corinthians 10:17). But when James combines *boast* with the other term, *arrogance*, we can be sure it's negative, especially since he identifies it as evil!

✦ How does boastful arrogance (or arrogant boasting) tie in to what James is teaching here?

✦ The remedy, James advises, whenever we make plans, is to say, "If the Lord wills . . ." (v. 15). He isn't giving us a few religious words to include when we talk about where we're going or what we expect to do. Remember, James is concerned with an attitude more than an activity. As you look at verses 15–16 together, what attitude is he commending?

✦ Making plans without a conscious focus on the Lord is something we've all done— or perhaps do regularly! And if we're honest, it might seem as though James is being just a tad too harsh about it all. The reason for James's strong language is what underlies arrogant boasting—a sense of self-sufficiency. Why do you think that self-sufficiency is incompatible with living the Christian life?

3. NO COASTING (4:17)

Guilty! That's all we can say in response to what James writes in verse 17: "Whoever knows the right thing to do and fails to do it, for him it is sin." Theologians call this sort of sin "sins of omission." To omit is to leave something undone, right? Sins of omission stand in contrast to "sins of commission," which are the sinful things we actively do.

✦ Given the immediate context (what James has been saying in verses 13–17), what sin of omission do you think is likely in view here in verse 17?

"When God, in infinite wisdom and fathomless love, ruins our plans, he means for his people to welcome it with trust and even joy. So, we say, 'If the Lord wills,' knowing our God will ultimately decide tomorrow."[25]

✦ Identify the "sins of omission" that Jesus pinpoints in the following passages:

· Matthew 25:31–46

· Luke 19:11–23

✦ James has been showing us throughout the letter what faithful discipleship looks like: controlling our tongue, embracing the poor and marginalized, and guarding against worldly influences. But which of us measures up to these standards? We don't always speak up to silence slander or to offer timely words of encouragement. We don't always make time to help a needy family or comfort a lonely widow. We don't always choose the path of holiness. We omit a good many things we should do! How does circling back to 4:6–10 show us our solution to this dilemma?

LET'S TALK

1. James tells us that we ought to say, "If the Lord wills," when we make a future plan, but we aren't required to take his words literally, automatically uttering those words, like when people say "bless you" after someone sneezes. How then are we to apply James's instructions?

2. Discuss why humility before the Lord is a necessary attitude not only to make plans for the future but to live out even the little daily goals we set. Describe how such humility would play out practically over the course of a typical day.

WOES AND WONDERS

JAMES 5:1-12

Many of us are familiar with the name Gordon Gekko. For others, the name rings a bell, but we can't quite place it. And then, of course, are those who've never heard of him. If you're in that latter group, that's perfectly okay, because he isn't a real person. Gordon Gekko was a lead character, a wealthy financier, in the 1987 movie *Wall Street*. Actor Michael Douglas did a good job portraying the greedy, devious Gekko (did you pick up on the fact that he has the name of a lizard?). He trampled on anyone who challenged his power and personal empire with no apologies, because Gordon Gekko practiced what he preached: "Greed, for lack of a better word, is good," he said. "Greed is right, greed works. Greed clarifies, cuts through, and captures the essence of the evolutionary spirit. Greed, in all its forms—greed for life, for money, for love, knowledge—has marked the upward surge of mankind."[26] Well, in this week's study, James has some really sharp words for people like Gordon Gekko. Afterward, James offers encouragement to suffering believers, whether the suffering is due to the fallout from people like Gekko or for other reasons. Whatever the source of suffering, James calls us to persevere with patience, with kindness to our brothers and sisters in Christ, and with hope—because the Lord is faithful to deliver his people.

1. GRABBING FOR GOLD (5:1-6)

James has sharp words for the wealthy, for the real-life Gordon Gekkos. It's important that we note how James's rebuke isn't directed to all rich people—just certain ones. He's calling out wealthy landowners, specifically those who don't know Christ. We know from elsewhere in God's word that being wealthy isn't sinful. The sheer number of godly rich people in the Bible makes that clear, figures such as Abraham, Job, David, Joseph of Arimathea, and very likely Lydia.[27] So in light of these examples, we know James's criticism isn't really about the money.

✤ Given that James's words are directed to unbelievers, what danger do you think James is warning about in verses 1–6?

....

....

....

....

✤ In verses 2 and 3, James describes what eventually happens to the possessions people accumulate, and it seems he based his words here on Jesus's teaching. Read what Jesus said in Matthew 6:19–21. How do his words explain what underlies James's criticism?

....

....

....

....

James accuses these wealthy unbelievers of laying up treasure "in the last days" (v. 3). When are these "last days"? Those days are actually *our* days. We are living in the last days, and so did those to whom James originally wrote. When the Son of God took on flesh and came to earth, he—Jesus Christ—lived for thirty-three years and then died on the cross for sinners. God raised him from the dead, and forty days later, Jesus ascended back into heaven, where he's seated at the Father's right hand. His coming to earth, followed by his death and resurrection and return to heaven, was the pivotal point of history. That's when the *last days* began, and we've been living in them ever since. So whenever we see this expression, "the last days," in the New Testament, it's describing not only the era of the apostles and those early Christians but our era too.

And the term implies a warning—the end is near, the time when Jesus will return to gather his people and to judge the wicked.

✦ What words or terms do you see in verses 1–6 that foreshadow the final judgment?

✦ You might wonder why James addresses unbelievers in a letter he's writing to his brothers and sisters in Christ, but there are some good reasons. One reason is that James's words could circle back to some of these wealthy unbelievers he's writing about so they'd be convicted to repent of their sin. Very likely, James also meant to encourage believers, especially those who were struggling to make ends meet or who were tempted to envy the wealthy. Read Psalm 73. What encouraged the psalmist in similar circumstances?

✦ James begins to zero in on the specific sins of these wealthy unbelievers. What specific sin does he pinpoint in verse 4, and why was this so bad? Take a look at God's law in Leviticus 19:13 and Deuteronomy 24:14 to help you answer.

> *"Even if we are not ripe for judgment, we need to know how God sees the lifestyle that leads to judgment. Further, no Christian is entirely immune to the sins James describes. . . . But we are prone to use power to gain an advantage over others (5:4). We are all tempted to use whatever riches we have in self-indulgent ways (5:5). So everyone needs James's warnings."*[28]

✦ James refers to God as "the Lord of hosts" in verse 4, a name for God that can also be translated as "Lord of heaven's armies." What do you think James is conveying about the Lord in this verse?

James details more sin in verse 5: "You have lived on the earth in luxury and in self-indulgence. You have fattened your hearts in a day of slaughter." That same expression—"the day of slaughter"—is found elsewhere in God's word to describe the final judgment (you might want to take a look at Jeremiah 12:1–3 and Revelation 19:17–21). As we noted earlier, being wealthy isn't sinful, nor is enjoying some luxuries, but clearly something is very wrong here.

✦ What do you see in each of the following passages that can make our experience of day-to-day things either a joyous blessing or a sinful indulgence?

· Philippians 3:18–19

· 1 Timothy 5:5–6

· 1 Timothy 6:17–19

· 2 Timothy 3:1–5

James finishes this very sobering section with what is likely a figurative rather than a literal pronouncement: "You have condemned and murdered the righteous person. He does not resist you" (v. 6). Worst of all, these unbelievers have used their wealth—and the worldly power that typically accompanies it—to drive the poor to the brink of starvation and homelessness. Back in James's day, the poor found little help in the legal system because it wasn't rooted in justice or fairness. The powerful determined the laws and worked the system to get their way. If they wanted someone's land, or if they didn't feel like paying wages to their laborers, well, they'd find a way to manipulate the courts in their favor. In the process, they accumulated more and more wealth and increasingly crushed the poor.

2. WAIT FOR THE LORD (5:7–12)

James turns his attention from the unrighteous rich back to God's own people, in this case, the poor who are being oppressed. He encourages them to hold on to their faith, even when they are suffering unjustly, until the Lord returns on judgment day to set things right. James uses farm imagery to stress the need for patience, imagery his readers would have resonated with. The rains in ancient Palestine, where James and his readers lived, were generally quite predictable. Seed was sown in the fall, just before the typical autumn rains began, which guaranteed that the seed would take deep root. And then more rain came in the spring, just before harvest, leading to lush, abundant crops. The Old Testament prophets mention these predictable rains too, as a way to showcase the Lord's favor and kindness (you can see for yourself in Jeremiah 5:24 and Joel 2:23).

✛ In verse 8, James instructs these suffering believers to "establish" their hearts because the Lord could return to deliver them at any time. Read Psalm 37, which may well have guided James's words here, and list several ways (if you find more than five, continue your list in the margins!) that the psalm shows how we establish our hearts as we wait for him.

1.

2.

3.

4.

5.

We are susceptible to certain temptations especially during seasons of suffering. One of those is grumbling, which James warns about in verse 9. Grumbling is a good catch-all word that covers a lot of verbal ground—complaining, criticizing, slander, and just all-around negative speech. In verse 9 James warns against uttering negative words about our brothers and sisters in Christ, because, he says, "the Judge is standing at the door." But wait a minute—these are believers he's addressing now, not the unbelievers of verses 1–6. How do we make sense of this? The truth is, judgment day will come to all, but what believers experience on that day will be tremendously different from what will happen to those who aren't united to Christ: "Christians will not face God's wrath on judgment day, but we will face God's assessment of every word and every deed."[29]

✦ To reinforce his encouragement to wait for the Lord, James draws from some Old Testament examples in verses 10 and 11. Read Hebrews 11:32–38, which outlines some of what those prophets experienced. What enabled them to persevere in the face of horrible mistreatment?

....

....

....

....

✦ James also guides us to consider Job, who endured the loss of every earthly blessing—his livelihood, his family, and his health. James holds up Job as an example of "steadfastness" (v. 11). Your Bible translation might use the word *perseverance*, *patience*, or *endurance*. What do you see in the passages below that made Job steadfast?

· Job 1:21–22

....

....

....

· Job 2:9–10

....

....

....

✦ What does James tell us about the Lord in verse 11, and how is it evidenced at the end of Job's ordeal? See Job 42:10–17.

3. JUST YES OR NO (5:12)

James seems to change the subject in verse 12, where he returns to matters of the tongue: "But above all, my brothers, do not swear, either by heaven or by earth or by any other oath, but let your 'yes' be yes and your 'no' be no, so that you may not fall under condemnation." Bible scholars aren't sure whether this verse ties in with what he has just said or whether it's more overarching, sort of wrapping up all he's said so far in the letter about the tongue.

✦ Whatever James's intention, we know he isn't forbidding any kind of oath-taking here. Even the apostle Paul took the occasional oath (see, for example, 2 Corinthians 1:23 or Philippians 1:8). James is most likely drawing from what Jesus said on the same subject. Read Jesus's teaching in Matthew 5:33–37. How do Jesus's words there (especially in verse 37) help us understand the point James is making?

LET'S TALK

1. James paints a picture of a patient farmer waiting for his crops to grow, and he calls us to have that same outlook as we wait for God to provide what we need. "Establish your hearts," James tells us, "for the coming of the Lord is at hand" (v. 8). We examined Psalm 37 alongside James's words. As you consider what James and the psalmist said, describe how you can personally apply what they say in order to establish your own heart.

2. James nails it—grumbling is easy to do when we are experiencing suffering. Why do you think we find ourselves so easily irritated and prone to judge or criticize people we love during a difficult season? Discuss how the grumbling trap can be avoided—concrete ways to recognize particular triggers and plans to avoid them. Consider also how to repair any relational brokenness that might have occurred as a result of your own grumbling.

PRAYING WITH POWER

JAMES 5:13-20

It's amazing what can go wrong with your body in just 5 seconds. I found out firsthand when I regained consciousness after a bad car accident years ago. Broken bones and layers of flesh scraped off down to the bone in some places made for a long, painful recovery. And there were setbacks along the way. My right elbow sustained one of the deepest wounds, and an infection set in. Surgery was necessary, the doctors said one day, and it was scheduled for the next morning. All that infected tissue would need to be removed in order for the wound to properly heal. I was terrified, of course, especially after learning what the surgery entailed, and I poured out my fear to my mother, who walked this painful journey with me. She listened to my tearful angst, and afterward she just leaned in and said a quiet prayer: "Lord, please heal this wound." Afterward we conversed about other things for about an hour. Suddenly, abruptly, my mother stopped what she was saying and exclaimed, "Look at your elbow!" The wound had visibly shrunk and was much less angry-red and oozy. When the doctor saw me the next morning, he seemed stumped, and perhaps a bit embarrassed. "Well, I guess we made a mistake," he said. "There's no infection here." What had happened? My mother and I knew. The Lord had answered her prayer. It's not that my mom has any sort of special healing gift. What she has is a strong, humble faith. God delights in and at times blesses such humility with powerfully tangible answers to prayer. We're going to find out more about trusting prayer this week as James instructs his readers to pour out their hearts to God on all occasions with all kinds of prayers. Afterward James finishes his letter with one final sobering, yet hope-filled instruction.

1. TIME TO PRAY (5:13–16)

"The only thing left to do at this point is pray." Have you ever heard someone say that? Maybe you've said it yourself. What we mean is that we've run out of ideas and practical means to fix the problem or advance the cause, but what we imply is that prayer is a last resort. However, as James shows us, when it comes to dealing with life's stuff—good or bad—prayer is the most practical thing we can do—and the most effective.

✦ What specific circumstances does James identify for prayer in verses 13–16, and what type of prayer does he attach to each circumstance?

Circumstance	Type of Prayer
1.	
2.	
3.	

James's instructions for anointing with oil weren't for medicinal purposes. The reason was spiritual. To get the idea, we have to go back to the Old Testament where oil was used to anoint people when they were being set apart for special ministry. The oil symbolized the Spirit of God coming to rest upon them in order to serve God in some special way (an example is Aaron the priest in Exodus 29:5–9). So here in James, the anointing by oil is meant to symbolize that the sick person "is being set apart for God's special attention and care."[30]

✦ How does 1 Peter 5:1–3 help us understand why elders—the church leaders—are the ones called to pray for and anoint the sick person?

....

....

....

There's lots of misunderstanding about James's words in verse 15, so it's important that we get what he's saying—and what he's not saying. When he writes that "the prayer of faith will save the one who is sick," James *is* saying that God blesses the strong faith of praying elders with healing. James is *not* saying that strong faith guarantees healing or that people stay sick because of weak faith. In other words, faith isn't magic, and it's most definitely not a bumper sticker—"What you believe, you can achieve." There's actually no power at all in faith. The power lies solely in the one in whom that faith is placed. In other words, faith doesn't heal. Only God does. When James speaks about the sick one being *saved* and *raised up*, he could have in mind physical healing or spiritual healing or perhaps both kinds.

✦ James makes a link in this section between sickness and sin. In order to make the best sense of this link here, read both John 9:1–3 and 1 Corinthians 11:28–30 and write a summary statement.

....

....

....

....

✦ James expands the call to pray in verse 16 from elders to all believers and urges us to confess our sins to others. How we go about confessing depends on the situation. "We confess private sins privately to the one or the few we offended. We confess public sins (which offend many) publicly."[31] How does each of the following passages help us understand why being honest about our sin can promote healing of all kinds—physical, spiritual, and relational?

· Proverbs 28:13

....

....

....

· Galatians 6:1–2

....

....

....

· 1 John 1:7

....

....

....

✦ James says in verse 16 that the prayers of righteous people are powerful. How does what James wrote back in 2:21–23 help us understand what he means by *righteous* here?

....

....

....

....

2. SOMEONE LIKE US (5:17-18)

James draws from the life of the Old Testament prophet Elijah to illustrate how God works through the prayer of someone righteous.

✦ Why do you think James identifies Elijah not as a prophet but as "a man with a nature like ours"?

....

....

....

....

✦ Elijah's prayer for rain brought to an end a very long drought in Israel. The drought and the sin that caused it are recorded for us in 1 Kings 17–18, along with how the Lord worked powerfully through Elijah during this time. Skim through the 1 Kings passage and jot down where you observe the principles of prayer that James is emphasizing.

....

....

....

....

Cessationism

Cessationists believe that some of the spiritual gifts that were active during Bible times—prophecies, miraculous healings, and speaking in tongues—ceased when the apostles died. That's because those gifts were meant to be signs, revelations of God's power in the gospel. Once the work of Jesus was finished—his life on earth, his death on the cross, and his resurrection and ascension back to heaven—the church grew and became established under the authority of the apostles as they attested to the truth of Jesus with signs and wonders. The apostles' words became part of Scripture, God's written revelation. After all that, there was no more need for those signs—those spiritual gifts—because all they'd pointed to had been fully revealed. That certainly doesn't mean that the Spirit can't heal people in unexpected ways when we pray for them. He does! And the Spirit still speaks today—he just does it through the preaching and teaching of the Bible. The Spirit also continues to work powerful providences in our lives in a variety of ways.[32]

3. WANDERER'S RESTORATION (5:19-20)

James's final words are different from other New Testament letters. He doesn't end with a word of blessing—a benediction—nor does he send personal greetings. Instead, he gives one last instruction for how to help a Christian brother or sister who has stopped walking faithfully with the Lord.

✦ Skim back through the letter to refresh your memory about the overarching themes in James's letter. With those in mind, how might we understand the wanderer of verse 19?

....

....

....

....

✦ A wanderer restored receives a two-part blessing, James says in verse 19. First, the wanderer is saved from spiritual death; and, second, his sins are covered. How do the following passages help us understand both parts of this blessing?

· Psalm 32:1–11

....

....

....

· 2 Corinthians 13:5–6

....

....

....

· Galatians 6:1–2

· 1 Peter 4:8

So as we come to the end of our study, what have we learned? James has set out for us the marks of true religion. Those marks are (1) the words we say, (2) the care we show to the poor and marginalized, and (3) keeping our hearts and lives from worldly pollution. The problem is, none of us lives up to these standards, right? We sin with our tongue, we're selfish with our resources, and we get so easily pulled into worldly pleasures at the expense of holiness. But thankfully James doesn't leave us there in our failure. He tells us this truth about our amazing God: "He gives more grace" (4:6). And then James shows us how we experience this grace, the way out of the messes we make:

> *But he gives more grace.* Therefore it says, "God opposes the proud but gives grace to the humble." Submit yourselves therefore to God. Resist the devil, and he will flee from you. Draw near to God, and he will draw near to you. Cleanse your hands, you sinners, and purify your hearts, you double-minded. Be wretched and mourn and weep. Let your laughter be turned to mourning and your joy to gloom. Humble yourselves before the Lord, and he will exalt you. (4:6–10)

That is grace—that is the gospel according to James. Amen.

LET'S TALK

1. How's your prayer life? Would you say that it's vibrant, or does it feel more like a chore? Discuss what you learned about prayer from our study this week and how you think it can make a difference in your own prayer life.

2. Do you have a trusted friend with whom you can be honest about your sin struggles and failures and share openly on a regular basis? Describe how it has made a difference in your spiritual growth. If you don't have such a friend, are you willing to prayerfully seek one out or ask someone to hold this trusted place in your life? If not, what hinders you?

3. As we come to the end of James, note what you've learned or what's affected you most about:

   · the character of God:

           · the gospel of salvation through Jesus Christ:

· the path of discipleship:

HELPFUL RESOURCES
FOR STUDYING JAMES

Doriani, Daniel M. *James*. Reformed Expository Commentary. Phillipsburg, NJ: P&R, 2007.

Guthrie, Nancy, and Daniel Doriani. "Dan Doriani on James." *Help Me Teach the Bible* podcast, August 2015. The Gospel Coalition. https://www.thegospelcoalition.org/.

Moo, Douglas J. *The Letter of James*. Pillar New Testament Commentary. Grand Rapids, MI: Eerdmans, 2000.

NOTES

1. Douglas J. Moo, *The Letter of James*, Pillar New Testament Commentary (Grand Rapids, MI: Eerdmans, 2000), 27.
2. "The Setting of James" map, taken from page 2388 of the *ESV® Study Bible* (The Holy Bible, English Standard Version®), copyright © 2008 by Crossway. Used by permission. All rights reserved.
3. Moo, *The Letter of James*, 46.
4. Daniel M. Doriani, *James*, Reformed Expository Commentary (Phillipsburg, NJ: P&R, 2007), 26.
5. Doriani, *James*, 32.
6. Doriani, *James*, 15.
7. Doriani, *James*, 49.
8. Bethany L. Jenkins, "Hearing and Doing: James 1:19–27," in *ESV Women's Devotional Bible*, ESV® Bible (Wheaton, IL: Crossway, 2014), 1512, accessed August 2, 2021, https://www.esv.org/resources/esv-womens-devotional-bible-online.
9. *ESV® Study Bible* (Wheaton, IL: Crossway, 2008), s.v. Matt. 5:5.
10. Doriani, *James*, 65.
11. Moo, *The Letter of James*, 108–9.
12. Moo, *The Letter of James*, 117.
13. Sinclair Ferguson, "The Tongue, the Bridle, and the Blessing: An Exposition of James 3:1–12," Desiring God website, September 26, 2008, https://www.desiringgod.org/.
14. Paul David Tripp, "War of Words," in *The Power of Words and the Wonder of God*, ed. John Piper and Justin Taylor (Wheaton, IL: Crossway, 2008), 30.
15. Ferguson, "The Tongue, the Bridle, and the Blessing."
16. Moo, *The Letter of James*, 166.
17. Mukesh Mani, "36 Inspirational Quotes on Why You Should Put Yourself First," Out of Stress website, June 27, 2020, https://www.outofstress.com/.
18. *ESV® Study Bible* (Wheaton, IL: Crossway, 2008), s.v. James 3:13.

19. Erik Thoennes, "Redeeming Jealousy: The Glory of God's Exclusive Love," Desiring God website, July 15, 2019, https://www.desiringgod.org.

20. Doriani, *James*, 135.

21. Doriani, *James*, 134.

22. Moo, *The Letter of James*, 196.

23. See *ESV® Study Bible*, s.vv. James 4:11 and 4:12.

24. Marshall Segal, "Few Are the Plans of Many: The Wisdom in Scheduling Well," Desiring God website, March 2, 2020, https://www.desiringgod.org/.

25. Segal, "Few Are the Plans of Many."

26. *Wall Street*, directed by Oliver Stone (1987; 20th Century Fox).

27. Find clues about their wealth here: Abraham's (Genesis 13:2–6); Job's (Job 1:1–3); David's (1 Chronicles 29:26–28); and Lydia's (Acts 16:14–15).

28. Doriani, *James*, 166.

29. Doriani, *James*, 181.

30. Moo, *The Letter of James*, 242.

31. Doriani, *James*, 200.

32. For more information about cessationism, you might want to check out Robert Rothwell, "Cessationism," *TableTalk* magazine, April 2020, https://tabletalkmagazine.com/article/2020/04/cessationism/. Another resource is Thomas Schreiner, "Why I Am a Cessationist," The Gospel Coalition website, January 2014, https://www.thegospelcoalition.org/.

Flourish Bible Study Series

For more information, visit **crossway.org**.